COURAGEOUS LEADERSHIP PROFILE

A Program for Using Courage to Transform the Workplace

BILL TREASURER
Author of *Courage Goes to Work*

LITTLE LEAPS
PRESS

For additional copies/bulk purchases of this book, please contact Giant Leap Consulting at 800-867-7239 or info@giantleapconsulting.com

Profile ISBN 978-1-948058-17-9

INSTRUCTIONS

Below you will find thirty statements that describe different dimensions of courageous behavior. Read each statement carefully, and then circle the number to the right of the statement that best reflects the degree to which you agree or disagree with each statement. Every statement must have a rating.

> **5 = Strongly Agree**
>
> **4 = Agree**
>
> **3 = Neither Agree Nor Disagree**
>
> **2 = Disagree**
>
> **1 = Strongly Disagree**

1	I like to try new ways of doing things, even though they may be risky.	1	2	3	4	5
2	I express my opinions to others, regardless of their position in the organization.	1	2	3	4	5
3	I believe that nearly all people at work have positive motives.	1	2	3	4	5
4	I have little difficulty trusting the people I work with.	1	2	3	4	5
5	I openly express my concerns when policies and procedures do not make sense.	1	2	3	4	5
6	I believe it is better to try something new and fail than to avoid attempting new things altogether.	1	2	3	4	5
7	I confront people who do not treat me or others fairly, regardless of their position in the organization.	1	2	3	4	5
8	I believe that individuals designated as leads of teams or projects to which I am assigned will make the right decisions.	1	2	3	4	5
9	I often come forward with improvement suggestions at work.	1	2	3	4	5
10	I often volunteer for new assignments even though I do not know all the details.	1	2	3	4	5
11	I believe people will not share information that I give them in confidence.	1	2	3	4	5
12	I am a real "go-getter"!	1	2	3	4	5
13	If I make a significant mistake, I quickly inform my boss.	1	2	3	4	5
14	If I experience a setback, I work persistently to correct what went wrong.	1	2	3	4	5
15	I am comfortable attempting new tasks with little or no supervision.	1	2	3	4	5

5 = Strongly Agree

4 = Agree

3 = Neither Agree Nor Disagree

2 = Disagree

1 = Strongly Disagree

16	I believe my co-workers do not intentionally do things to offend me.	1	2	3	4	5
17	I voice my opinions, even though they may be unpopular with others.	1	2	3	4	5
18	I let my boss know when I do not agree with his or her decisions or directives.	1	2	3	4	5
19	When things go wrong, my first priority is to understand *why* they went wrong, rather than *who* was at fault.	1	2	3	4	5
20	I prefer jobs that provide me with a variety of non-routine tasks.	1	2	3	4	5
21	I enjoy stepping out of my comfort zone to learn new skills.	1	2	3	4	5
22	I am assertive when dealing with intimidating people at work.	1	2	3	4	5
23	I do not micromanage because I know that people will make the right decisions without frequent intervention on my part.	1	2	3	4	5
24	I believe that my co-workers have good intentions when they provide me with negative feedback about my performance.	1	2	3	4	5
25	I prefer embracing change to resisting it.	1	2	3	4	5
26	I speak as openly to people in positions of authority as I do with my co-workers.	1	2	3	4	5
27	I am sure that my co-workers will do what they say they will do.	1	2	3	4	5
28	I am a trusting person at work.	1	2	3	4	5
29	I am an assertive person at work.	1	2	3	4	5
30	I volunteer to lead assignments that others tend to shy away from.	1	2	3	4	5

COURAGEOUS LEADERSHIP
PROFILE SCORING

Instructions:

1. Transfer the answers (numbers) you gave for each item to the scoring framework below. Place the numeric scores in the appropriate spaces below. Note that the numbers below are not in sequential order.

2. Add the columns and fill in the totals within the light-gray shaded areas inside the buckets.

TRY	*TRUST*	*TELL*
1._____	3._____	2._____
6._____	4._____	5._____
10._____	8._____	7._____
12._____	11._____	9._____
14._____	16._____	13._____
15._____	19._____	17._____
20._____	23._____	18._____
21._____	24._____	22._____
25._____	27._____	26._____
30._____	28._____	29._____
TRY Total	*TRUST Total*	*TELL Total*

TRY   TRUST   TELL

COURAGEOUS LEADERSHIP PROFILE INTERPRETATION

	LOW	MEDIUM	HIGH
	Score of 10 to 23	Score of 24 to 37	Score of 38 to 50
TRY	People with mostly empty TRY buckets are comfortable when they are working within established guidelines and systems. They may resist bold steps, even when a new approach is needed. They prefer to implement systems that support their traditions and history.	People with partially full TRY buckets work to stretch themselves when they have good evidence that the risk can be controlled. They often prefer to implement evolutionary approaches to new problems.	People with full TRY buckets are willing to experiment with new approaches. They are willing to fail publicly and see failure as an opportunity to seek self-improvement or system improvement. They prefer to implement revolutionary approaches to new problems.
TRUST	People with mostly empty TRUST buckets hesitate to share information, believing that "knowledge is power." They often are uncomfortable allowing others to take on important tasks in their areas of expertise, preferring to do it themselves.	People with partially full TRUST buckets share information related to work activities, but often withhold any data that may appear to weaken their positions or standing. They tend to double-check the work of others.	People with full TRUST buckets are comfortable sharing work-related and personal information with others. They often allow others to "own their own scope" and intervene only when someone else asks for help.
TELL	People with mostly empty TELL buckets feel apprehension at the idea of "crossing the line" and frequently hold back when they should make their thoughts and feelings known.	People with partially full TELL buckets assert themselves when they feel that they can add value. They are often careful to have their facts straight before offering their views and may withhold clearly unpopular opinions.	People with full TELL buckets speak freely and candidly—even when the news is not good or simply unconventional. They are comfortable giving and receiving information that runs counter to popular opinion.

COURAGEOUS LEADERSHIP PROFILE STRATEGIES TO INCREASE YOUR BUCKET

TRY	Write on a piece of paper the areas at work in which you are playing it too safe. In each instance, identify the costs to your career for playing it too safe.
	Take "little leaps" as a way to move toward bigger ones. Experiment in small ways, such as taking a new route to work each week or eating at a new restaurant.
	Write down examples of daring actions that you've taken in the past. How did you feel before taking the action? Afterward? What lessons can you apply from previous actions in your current circumstances?
	When facing a risk, identify the risks of not taking it. What are the risks of *in*action?
TRUST	Before attempting to fill your trust bucket, list a few examples of when you have been betrayed in the past. Often people are slow to trust because they have been burned in the past.
	Identify the negative impact that having low levels of trust is having on your career or work relationships. Also identify how filling your trust bucket might benefit you.
	Identify the criteria that you apply before trusting someone. Complete the following statement, "I will trust you when. . ." Next, identify how well you live up to the criteria that you use to trust others. Do you trust yourself?
	List five things that people do that *build* trust. Now list five things that people do that *break* trust. For the next week keep track of how often you exhibit either trust *builders* or *trust breakers.*
	Apply active listening when interacting with others. Before having your needs met, take an interest in understanding the other person's challenges and being supportive of him or her.
	"Trust first," which means that, instead of having people "prove" themselves to you, start by giving them your trust.
TELL	Identify a few examples of when you bit your tongue and regretted doing so. Why did you bite your tongue? Why did you regret it? If you could relive those examples (without being afraid or uncomfortable), what would you have done differently?
	Typically people have more difficulty *tell*ing things to their bosses than to their co-workers or direct reports. Ask your boss whether he or she wants you to be a "yes" person. Most bosses will tell you that they *don't* want you to be a brown-noser. Once you have an agreement, refer back to it when you need to disagree with your boss.
	Prepare. Use "linguistic precision," that is, strategize (by writing down) the *exact* message that you want to convey. You'll have far greater success than if you just wing it.
	Practice. Rehearse what you want to say with someone with whom you have high levels of trust.
	A lot of people become nervous and flustered when they speak assertively. This is the best evidence that you are being courageous!

LEADERSHIP DEVELOPMENT PLAN

The *Courageous Leadership* Development Plan (CLDP) can be used to help you process what you've learned by completing the *Courageous Leadership* Profile. Simply answer the questions below to better understand what role courage is playing in your career, and where your opportunities to demonstrate more career courage may be.

Name: Manager:

Position: Date of Assessment:

Organization:

Personal Career Aspirations: **What do you aim to achieve in your career?**	• • •
Notable Career Successes: **What successes that you've already had in your career do you feel most proud of?**	• • •

STRENGTHS

WHAT ARE YOUR STRENGTHS IN EACH BUCKET?	
 **TRY** Strengths	• • •
 **TRUST** Strengths	• • •
 **TELL** Strengths	• • •

AREAS TO DEVELOP

What are your improvement opportunities in each bucket?	
TRY Improvements	• • •
TRUST Improvements	• • •
TELL Improvements	• • •

PERSONAL COURAGE STATEMENT

In the space below, write down what you hope to achieve by putting more courage to work. When it comes to courage, what are you "all about?"

COURAGEOUS LEADERSHIP ACTION PLAN

In the next section, identify some Courage Goals, and include how you will measure success in the short term (ST) and long term (LT). Also set a date when you first plan on reviewing the progress you've made toward your Courage Goals.

GOAL 1				
Measure(s) of Success	• • •	Goal Review Dates:	ST	LT
GOAL 2				
Measure(s) of Success	• • •	Goal Review Dates:	ST	LT
GOAL 3				
Measure(s) of Success	• • •	Goal Review Dates:	ST	LT

THE BIG PICTURE

What personal outcomes am I seeking by working on my courageous behavior?

_____

_____

_____

_____

_____

How can my supervisor help me develop my courageous behavior?

_____

_____

_____

_____

_____

What other resources should I deploy to develop my courageous behavior?

_____

_____

_____

_____

_____

Other thoughts:

_____

_____

_____

_____

_____

COURAGE NOTES

COURAGE NOTES

_____
_____
_____
_____
_____
_____
_____
_____
_____
_____
_____
_____
_____
_____
_____
_____
_____
_____
_____
_____
_____
_____
_____
_____
_____

COURAGE NOTES

_____
_____
_____
_____
_____
_____
_____
_____
_____
_____
_____
_____
_____
_____
_____
_____
_____
_____
_____
_____
_____
_____
_____
_____
_____

COURAGE NOTES

ADDITIONAL COURAGE RESOURCES

Books About Courage

Blumenthhal, Noah. *Be the Hero* (Berrett-Koehler, 2009).

Brown, Brené. *Daring Greatly* (Avery, 2012).

Center for Courage & Renewal, *The Courage Way* (Berrett-Koehler, 2018).

Chaleff, Ira. *The Courageous Follower* (2nd ed.) (Berrett-Koehler, 2003).

Duckworth, Angela. *Grit* (Scribner, 2016).

Kennedy, Caroline. *Profiles in Courage for Our Times* (Hyperion, 2003).

Kennedy, John F. *Profiles in Courage* (HarperCollins, 2006; original edition, 1956).

Klien, M. and Napier, R. *The Courage to Act* (Davies-Black, 2003).

Kouzes, James M. and Posner, Barry Z. *Finding the Courage to Lead* (Jossey-Bass, 2013).

Lee, Gus. *Courage* (Jossey-Bass, 2006).

McCain, John. *Why Courage Matters* (Random House, 2004).

Sutton, Robert. *The No Asshole Rule* (Warner Business Books, 2007).

Treasurer, Bill. *Courage Goes to Work* (Berrett-Koehler, 2008).

Treasurer, Bill. *Right Risk* (Berrett-Koehler, 2003).

Worrell, Margie. *Find Your Courage* (McGraw-Hill, 2008).

Articles

Lomenick, Brad. (2013). 6 Ways to be a More Courageous Leader. www.fastcompany.com.

Mahoney, J. (2002). Cultivating Moral Courage in Business. *Business Ethics: A European Review.*

Mascarella, Janene. (2008, November). No Backbone? Then It's High Time You Built One. *American Way Magazine*, p. 26.

Pearse, Susan. (2013). Courage, The Most Important Leadership Virtue. www.HuffingtonPost.com.

Stettner, Morey. (2008, November 23). Channel Worker Worries into Constructive Action. *Investor's Business Daily.*

Tardanica, Susan. (2013). 10 Traits of Courageous Leaders. www.forbes.com.

Tobak, Steve. (2013). 8 Ways to be a Courageous Leader. www.inc.com.

Treasurer, Bill. (2009, Spring). Courageous Leadership: Modeling the Way. *Leader-to-Leader*, pp. 13–17.

Treasurer, Bill. (2009, June). Courage Goes to Work: The Leader's Role in Building Backbone. *Leadership Excellence*, p. 14.

Worline, Monica. *Sustaining Courage in Trying Times.* www.bus.umich.edu/facultyresearch/research/TryingTimes/Courage.htm

Websites

www.be-the-hero.com

www.couragebuilding.com

www.couragegoestowork.com

www.courageousleadership.org (innovative leadership models and resources to develop women leaders)

www.couragerenewal.org

www.giantleapconsulting.com

www.ted.com (search for courage)

ABOUT THE AUTHOR

Bill Treasurer is the Chief Encouragement Officer at Giant Leap Consulting, a courage-building company that is on a mission to help people and organizations be more courageous, so they can drive out fear and produce exceptional results.

Bill is the author of *Courage Goes to Work* (Berrett-Koehler, 2008), an international bestseller about how to build workplace courage. Bill is also the creator of the world's only do-it-yourself courage-building training program, *Courageous Leadership: Using Courage to Transform the Workplace*. The program promotes leadership courage and has been taught to thousands of executives in eleven countries on four continents.

Bill is also the author of *A Leadership Kick in the Ass* (Berrett-Koehler, 2017), that highlights how critical it is that leaders make a "Holy Shift!" – shifting their attention from themselves to the people they're privileged to lead. Bill is also the author of *Leaders Open Doors* (ATD Press, 2014), which focuses on the key responsibility leaders have to be opportunity-creators. Bill donates 100% of the royalties from the book to programs that support children with special needs.

Bill's first book, *Right Risk* (Berrett-Koehler, 2003), is about smart risk taking and draws on Bill's experiences as a professional athlete. Bill is a former captain of the U.S. High Diving Team and has performed over 1,500 dives from heights that reached over 100 feet.

For over two decades, Bill has worked to help leaders be more courageous, just, and effective. His clients include NASA, eBay, Accenture, Lenovo, UBS Bank, Georgia Power, SPANX, the Pittsburgh Pirates, and the U.S. Department of Veterans Affairs. Bill has also facilitated strategic planning programs at renowned universities including Harvard, MIT, Yale, Brown, Cornell, USC, UC Berkeley, UMass, UPenn, and others. Bill attended West Virginia University on a full athletic scholarship and received his master's degree from the University of Wisconsin. Connect with Bill though social media: Facebook (http://facebook.com/bill.treasurer), Twitter (@btreasurer), and LinkedIn (www.linkedin.com/in/courage). Learn more at BillTreasurer.com.

ABOUT GIANT LEAP CONSULTING, INC.

Giant Leap Consulting (GLC) is a courage-building company that is on a mission to help people and organizations act with more courage. Since its founding in 2002, GLC has conducted over 1,000 client engagements to help individuals and organizations perform at a higher level. Our services include:

- **Courageous Future**: Strategic planning to rally the organization around a bold and compelling vision for the future.

- **Courageous Leadership**: Comprehensive leadership development and succession planning programs for emerging and experience leaders.

- **Courageous Teaming**: Team-building programs to strengthen and align senior executive teams.

- **Courageous Coaching**: Individual coaching to strengthen the leadership skills of managers and executives.

- **Courageous Development**: Skill-building training workshops for all employees, covering such topics as Culture, Leading Change, Professionalism, Team Leadership, Decision making and Risk taking, Presentation Skills, Strategic Thinking, and many others. We specialize in custom-designed workshops.

Giant Leap is proud of its client list, which includes NASA, Lenovo, eBay, Saks Fifth Avenue, Walsh Construction, Aldridge Electric Inc., SPANX, UBS Bank, Novo Nordisk, Plote Construction, the Pittsburgh Pirates, the CDC, and the U.S. Department of Veterans Affairs. Through our work with the National Science Foundation, we have facilitated strategic planning engagements at Harvard University, Massachusetts Institute of Technology (MIT), Yale University, the University of Massachusetts, University of California at Berkeley, University of Southern California (USC), Brown University, and many other renowned institutions of higher learning.

To learn more about Giant Leap Consulting, visit our websites:
www.GiantLeapConsulting.com, www.ManagerialCourage.com,
www.CourageBuilding.com, and www.LeadersOpenDoors.com.
To inquire about Giant Leap's services, send an email to info@giantleapconsulting.com
or call 800-867-7239.

www.ingramcontent.com/pod-product-compliance
Lightning Source LLC
Chambersburg PA
CBHW051235200326

41519CB00025B/7392